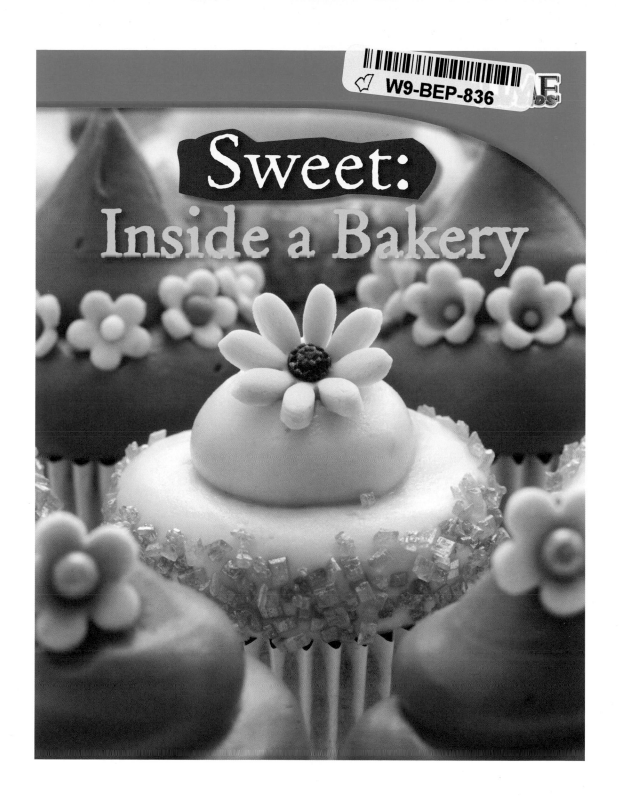

Sweet:
Inside a Bakery

Lisa Greathouse

Consultant

Timothy Rasinski, Ph.D.
Kent State University

Publishing Credits

Dona Herweck Rice, *Editor-in-Chief*

Robin Erickson, *Production Director*

Lee Aucoin, *Creative Director*

Conni Medina, M.A.Ed., *Editorial Director*

Jamey Acosta, *Editor*

Heidi Kellenberger, *Editor*

Lexa Hoang, *Designer*

Stephanie Reid, *Photo Editor*

Rachelle Cracchiolo, M.S.Ed., *Publisher*

Image Credits

Cover Ruth Black/Shutterstock; p.3 lazlo/Shutterstock; p.4-5 Oleg Golovnev/Shutterstock; p.4 top to bottom: brytta/Shutterstock; Andy Heyward/Shutterstock; p.5 Gordana Sermek/Shutterstock; p.6 George Muresan/Shutterstock; p.7 left to right: areashot/Shutterstock; Wavebreakmediamicro/Dreamstime; p.7 bottom: gerenme/iStockphoto; p.8 Claudia Dewald/iStockphoto; p.9 top to bottom: Subbotina Anna/Shutterstock; Dmitry Fisher/Shutterstock; p.10 goodgold99/Shutterstock; p.11 top inset: Robert Neumann/Shutterstock; p.11 bottom inset: wavebreakmedia ltd/Shutterstock; p.11 top: hidesy/iStockphoto; p.11-12 Mike Rodriguez/iStockphoto; p.12 Catalin Petolea/Shutterstock; p.13 inset: Oleksii Abramov/Shutterstock; p.13 Bryan Solomon/Shutterstock; p.14-15 Elena Schweitzer/Shutterstock; p.14 bottom Susan Ashukian/istockphoto; p.15 Louie Psihoyos/Corbis; p.15 inset: Artistic Endeavor/Shutterstock; p.16 top: Sam Yeh/AFP/Getty Images/Newscom; p.16 bottom: photovideostock/iStockphoto; p.17 top: James Steidl/Shutterstock; p.17 bottom: Tim Bradley; p.18 Ruth Black/Shutterstock; p.19 top: Dan Peretz/Shutterstock; p.19 bottom: Thomas M Perkins/Shutterstock; p.20-21 Nate A.; Amero/Shutterstock; p.20 inset: Lauri Patterson/iStockphoto; p.21 Marcel Jancovic/Shutterstock; p.22 Olga Utlyakova/Shutterstock; p.23 bottom: bonchan/Shutterstock; p.23 top: Sally Scott/Shutterstock; p.24 top to bottom: Carmen Steiner/Shutterstock; geniuscook_com/Shutterstock; Brian Weed/Shutterstock; Robyn Mackenzie/Shutterstock; p.25 top to bottom: Catalin Petolea/Shutterstock; highviews/Shutterstock; William Berry/Shutterstock; Komar Maria/Shutterstock; seroymac/Shutterstock; p.26 auremar/Shutterstock; p.27 top: Michael Gatewood/iStockphoto; p.27 inset: Jack Puccio/iStockphoto; p.28 Yuri Arcurs/Shutterstock; p.29 left to right Alexander Raths/Shutterstock; Bochkarev Photography/Shutterstock; p.29 inset: caracterdesign/iStockphoto; p.32 Subbotina Anna/Shutterstock; background: Wojtek Jarco/Shutterstock; Krisztina Farkas/Shutterstock; Scorpp/Shutterstock; wdstock; seanami; SDbT; bradwieland; LanceBLance/iStockphoto; back cover: Elena Schweitzer/Shutterstock

Based on writing from *TIME For Kids*.

TIME For Kids and the *TIME For Kids* logo are registered trademarks of TIME Inc. Used under license.

Teacher Created Materials

5301 Oceanus Drive
Huntington Beach, CA 92649-1030
http://www.tcmpub.com

ISBN 978-1-4333-3663-8

© 2012 Teacher Created Materials, Inc.
Made in China
Nordica.072017.CA21700826

Table of Contents

A Visit to the Bakery

Do you have a sweet tooth? Let's visit a **bakery**!

There is so much to choose from. There are cakes, cookies, and pies. You can find pastries and breads. And don't forget about the cupcakes. Yum! A sweet **aroma** greets you as you walk through the door. There are cinnamon rolls fresh from the oven.

Who Needs an Oven?

The art of baking dates back to ancient Egypt. The first baked good was probably a round, flat bread baked on a hot stone.

Glazed **doughnuts** and freshly brewed coffee line the shelves. Look inside the display case. Every shelf is full of deliciously sweet treats. But how do they make it all?

Baking is a process. Here, bakers knead the dough until it's just right.

The morning is the bakery's busiest time. The staff gets to work early—even before the sun rises! There is a lot of work to do before the bakery opens its doors for business.

The back room may be bigger than the front where the display cases are. In the back, giant mixers prepare dough and cake batter. Bakers roll dough on long countertops. Cakes and cupcakes are decorated with swirls of icing. Bakers slide wide pans of breads into huge ovens. The back of the bakery is where all the action is.

Mastering Measurements

It's important to make careful **measurements** when baking. Take time to learn what these common amounts look like. You'll be able to read a **recipe** and predict how it will taste before you make it.

1 teaspoon
1 tablespoon
1 cup
1 quart
1 gallon

A baker carefully weighs butter. The measurement has to be exact!

The Art of Baking Bread

By 4:00 A.M., bakers are measuring flour, **yeast**, water, and salt. These **ingredients** combine to make bread dough. Everything goes into a giant mixer. After the mixing is done, bakers use their hands or a machine to **knead** (NEED) the dough. They flatten, fold, push, and turn the dough.

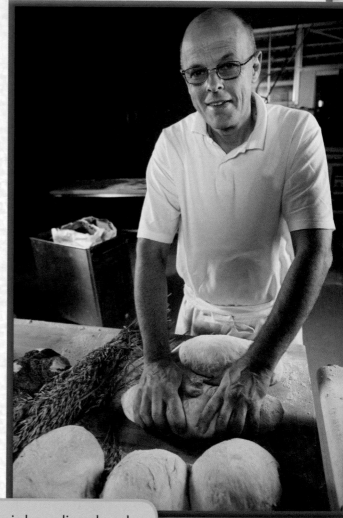

A baker is kneading dough.

Some breads take on interesting shapes. This dough looks like a spiral.

The Science of Bread Baking

There is a lot of science in the bakery. In fact, the yeast in bread dough is alive! Yeast is a kind of **fungus**. It reacts with the sugar in flour to create **carbon dioxide**. This makes the dough rise. Yeast can also give bread a light, airy **texture**.

After the dough rises, the baker shapes it. The bread can be placed in a loaf pan. Or it can be shaped into a long stick (like a **baguette**), a ring (like a bagel), or even a pretzel! The bread can be made in dozens of shapes. The dough is then allowed time to rise again before it goes in the oven. The temperature of the oven and the baking time depend on the dough's size and shape.

a bread slicer

The Greatest Thing Since Sliced Bread!

The next time you reach for a slice of bread to make a sandwich, think about this: It wasn't until 1928 that inventor Otto Frederick Rohwedder came up with a bread-slicing machine! Before then, people bought loaves and cut the slices themselves.

Flour Power

Flour is the main ingredient in bread making. White, wheat, whole grain, rye, sourdough, blended—there are as many different kinds of flour as there are breads!

There are many different kinds of dough. There is dough just for pastries and piecrust. This kind of dough has flour, salt, sugar, eggs, and butter. The butter, or **shortening**, gives it a flaky or crumbly texture. Because it does not have yeast like bread dough, it does not rise. It stays flat. That makes it easy to roll it thin with a **rolling pin**.

The bakery sells apple, cherry, and strawberry pies. Yum! Which is your favorite?

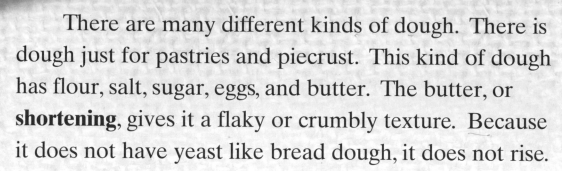

You can make your own piecrust at home.

Popular Pies

Apple pie is the perfect treat! This American favorite is especially popular in the summer and fall.

If you're really hungry, you can share it with a friend.

$\frac{1}{2}$

If you have two friends, you'll still have lots of pie.

$\frac{1}{3}$

You'll have a hearty dessert if four people share the pie.

$\frac{1}{4}$

What if 8 people want dessert? You'll have to cut smaller pieces.

$\frac{1}{8}$

If there's a party you can cut 16 small pieces. That's a recipe for success!

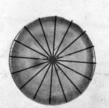

$\frac{1}{16}$

All this crust needs is a tasty filling and someone to eat it!

Sweet Treats

Chocolate chip. Oatmeal raisin. Sugar. Snickerdoodle. What would life be like without cookies?

Most cookie batters start with flour, eggs, sugar, and butter. But bakers can add many other ingredients. Candy, nuts, vanilla, and raisins are just a few tasty extras. Cookies can be iced and topped with sprinkles. Some bakeries sell a **dozen** kinds of cookies!

Cookie cutters come in lots of shapes, too. There are stars, hearts, snowflakes— even dog bones!

What other shapes could you cut a cookie into?

The Most Famous Cookie

Did you know the chocolate chip cookie was invented by accident? In 1930, Ruth Wakefield was mixing a batch of cookies for her guests at the Toll House Inn when she ran out of baker's chocolate. She put in pieces of a chocolate bar instead, and guests loved them. The chocolate chip cookie was born!

Did You Know?

In 2003, a baking company made the world's biggest cookie, measuring 102 feet in **diameter**. It took 40,000 pounds of ingredients to make the dough! What kind of cookie was it? Chocolate chip, of course!

102 feet

These cakes are almost too special to eat.

Getting Bigger...

There is no yeast in cake batter. So why does it rise as it bakes in the oven? The secret ingredient is **baking powder**. Baking powder releases carbon dioxide, too. That makes the cake fluffy.

Cakes Are King!

No party is complete without a cake. Lots of bakeries make creative cakes. People who design and decorate these cakes are not only bakers—they are artists, too!

Some people like their cakes to say something about who they are or their hobbies. Some cakes take the shape of dogs, birds, cars, trains, houses, pianos, and even robots. Every cake is a delicious work of art!

Wedding Cakes

The wedding cake plays a big role on a couple's big day. Some wedding cakes can be several feet high and have as many as six **tiers**! They can feature ribbons and flowers that look very real but are safe to eat.

cake topper

dowels

tier base

Cupcakes Are Big!

Cupcakes may be small, but they are a big business. In fact, some bakeries sell only cupcakes.

Years ago, most cupcakes were simple. They were made with vanilla or chocolate cake batter. They were frosted with vanilla or chocolate icing.

Today, the batter might be red velvet or carrot cake. Food coloring can make the icing just about any color. Some bakers fill their cupcakes with buttercream or fudge. And the toppings have come a long way—try sprinkles and marshmallows or fruit and crumbled candy bars!

Competitive Cupcakes

Cupcakes are so trendy that a hit reality TV show has cupcake bakers competing against each other. The baker whose cupcakes are judged to be the best is the winner!

Not Just Kid Stuff

Over 500 million cupcakes are enjoyed each year in the United States!

Nuts for Doughnuts

It's a simple round cake with a hole in the middle. But the doughnut is one of the bakery's biggest sellers.

Doughnuts are made with a skinny piece of dough in the shape of a ring. They are placed in hot oil and fried. There are yeast doughnuts and doughnuts made with cake batter. Some have no hole in the middle and are filled with jam or cream. Not all doughnuts are round. Some are long bars. Others are twisted. They can be topped with glaze, sprinkles, chocolate, nuts, sugar—or just about anything!

The Missing Piece

One of the most popular parts of the doughnut is the part that isn't even there! Bakers fry small ball-shaped pieces of dough and sell them as doughnut holes!

PIES INSID

CITY

BAKE

SH BRB

PIES
APPLE $14.00 – APRICOT
BLUEBERRY $14.50 Boysenberry
APPLE – RHUBARB

Doughnut Discovery

No one is sure who invented the doughnut. But it is believed that Dutch settlers brought the *olykoek*—meaning "sweet cake fried in fat"—to North America. These cakes had fruit in the middle. An American teenager working on a lime-trading ship in 1847 is believed to be the first to punch a hole in the center of the dough!

Muffin Madness

A muffin is like a cross between a cupcake and bread. It's not as sweet as a cupcake and does not have frosting. But unlike bread, muffins are made with a type of cake batter. The batter is poured into the cups of a muffin tin. The batter rises over the top of the cup. This gives the finished muffin a giant mushroom shape. Extras such as fruit, poppy seeds, and chocolate chips can be baked inside.

The Giant Muffin

Standard muffin tins have cups that are $2\frac{1}{2}$ inches across in diameter. But today, giant muffins are popular. The muffin tins for these have cups that are $3\frac{1}{4}$ inches in diameter.

Do You Know the Muffin Man?

Muffins have been popular since the 18th century. In England, muffin men would walk around carrying muffin tins on their heads and ringing their bells so that people would buy these delicious treats.

23

Around the World

People all over the world love bakeries. The most popular baked goods depend on which part of the world you are in. Which sweets look good to you?

Country	Baked Good	What It Is
Austria	sacher torte (SAH-ker TAWRT)	a double-layer chocolate cake with apricot-jam filling.
Australia	pavlova	a light cake with a crisp exterior and a soft marshmallow center
Denmark	Danish pastry	a buttery, flaky pastry folded into layers; it can be topped with chocolate, sugar, icing, jam, or custard
France	croissant (kruh-SAHNT)	a rich, buttery crescent-shaped roll

Country	Baked Good	What It Is
Germany	strudel (STROOD-l)	a cake shaped into a long roll and often filled with fruit and topped with icing
India	barfi (BER-fee)	flat and dense like cheesecake, made by cooking sugar and evaporated milk with a main ingredient, like nuts
Italy	biscotti (bih-SKOT-ee)	a long, dry, hard cookie that has been baked twice
Mexico	tres leches (TRESS LAY-chays)	a sweet, dense sponge cake soaked in three kinds of milk
Turkey	baklava (BAH-kluh-vah)	a rich, sweet pastry made of thin layers of dough filled with chopped nuts and syrup or honey

The Business of Baking

Running a successful bakery takes a lot more than great recipes. It takes a lot of business sense. Employees need to be hired. Equipment, supplies, and ingredients must be ordered. Coming up with the right menu takes careful planning. (Some bakeries serve soup, sandwiches, and smoothies, too.) A good **marketing** plan helps get the word out about the business. A website lets customers order online. Finally, **bookkeeping** and **budgeting** keep a business on track so it can pay its bills.

These bakers are hard at work making fresh goodies for you to enjoy.

Baker's Dozen

A dozen is 12 of something. But when you order a dozen doughnuts, you might wind up with 13. That's called a *baker's dozen*.

The Next Batch

Do you love spending time in the kitchen? Do you enjoy whipping up batches of cookies or baking pies? Do you like to watch TV shows about chefs creating amazing cakes? You might want to become a baker!

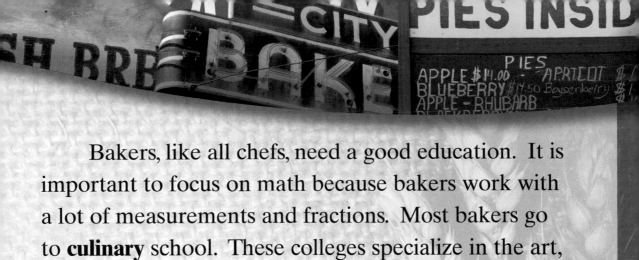

Bakers, like all chefs, need a good education. It is important to focus on math because bakers work with a lot of measurements and fractions. Most bakers go to **culinary** school. These colleges specialize in the art, science, math, and business of cooking and baking.

Who knows? Maybe you will develop the next great cookie recipe!

Watch, Learn, Bake!

Some bakers become **apprentices**. These are people who work with and learn from someone more experienced.

Glossary

apprentices—people who work for somebody else to learn that person's skill or trade

aroma—a pleasant smell

baguette—a long loaf of bread, originally made in France

bakery—a place where baked goods are made and sold

baking powder—a baking ingredient that releases carbon dioxide

bookkeeping—keeping records of the money taken in and paid out by a business

budgeting—keeping track of the amount of money to be spent for a certain period or purpose

carbon dioxide—a gas without color or odor that is made up of carbon and oxygen

culinary—anything related to cooking or baking

diameter—the width of a circle, sphere, or cylinder

doughnuts—skinny pieces of dough that are often formed into rings

dozen—12 of something

fungus—a living thing that cannot make its own food and eats plants, animals, and other living matter

ingredients—the parts of a mixture

knead—to mix by pressing, folding, and pulling

marketing—advertising and other activities aimed at selling or promoting a product or service

measurements—sizes, weights, or amounts of something

recipe—a list of ingredients and instructions for making a food dish

rolling pin—a long wooden or metal cylinder used to flatten dough

shortening—fat used in some baking

texture—the feel or look of a surface

tiers—rows or layers placed one above another

yeast—fungi used to make bread

Index

About the Author

Lisa Greathouse grew up in Brooklyn, N.Y., and graduated from the State University of New York at Albany with a bachelor's degree in English and journalism. She was a reporter, a writer, and an editor for The Associated Press for 10 years, covering news on everything from science and technology to business and politics. She has also been a magazine editor and a writer for education publications and a university website. Today, she works as a writer at the Disneyland Resort, where she oversees an employee magazine. In her spare time, she enjoys visiting Mickey Mouse and riding Space Mountain. She is married with two children and resides in Southern California.